I0411000

Contents

Acronyms

ACT Artemisinin Combination Therapies
AI Avian Influenza
AIDS Acquired Immune Deficiency Syndrome
ARI Acute Respiratory Infection
ARV Anti-retroviral drug
ASEAN Association of Southeast Asian Nations
AusAID Australian Agency for International Development
BEP US Department of State Biosecurity Engagement Program
CCM Country Coordinating Mechanism
CDC US Centers for Disease Control and Prevention
CSO Civil Society Organization
DOD Department of Defense Office of Defense Cooperation
DOTS Directly Observed Therapy, Short Course
EPT Emerging Pandemic Threat
e-TB Electronic Tuberculosis Manager
FAO Food and Agricultural Organization of the United Nations
FP Family Planning
G-20 Group of Twenty Finance Ministers and Central Bank Governors
GFATM Global Fund to Fight AIDS, Tuberculosis, and Malaria
GHI Global Health Initiative
GOI Government of Indonesia
HHS US Department of Health and Human Services
HIV Human Immunodeficiency Virus
HSS Health Systems Strengthening
HSWG Health Sector Working Group
IBBS Integrated Biological and Behavioral Survey
ICT Information, communication and technology
IDHS Indonesia Demographic and Health Survey
IHR International Health Regulations
IMR Infant Mortality Rate
IR Intermediate Result

JICA Japanese International Cooperation Agency
LF Lymphatic Filariasis
MCC Millennium Challenge Corporation
MCH Maternal and Child Health
M&E Monitoring and Evaluation
MDG Millennium Development Goal
MDR-TB Multi-Drug Resistant Tuberculosis
MMR Maternal Mortality Ratio
MOH Ministry of Health
NGO Non-Governmental Organization
NIAID National Institute of Allergy and Infectious Diseases
NIH National Institutes of Health
NMR Neonatal Mortality Rate
NTD Neglected Tropical Disease
NTP National TB Program
OR Operations Research
PEPFAR President's Emergency Plan for AIDS Relief
PLWHA People Living With HIV/AIDS
PMTCT Prevention of Mother-to-Child Transmission
PPP Public Private Partnership
RH/FP Reproductive Health and Family Planning
S&T Science and Technology
STH Soil Transmitted Helminthiasis
TA Technical Assistance
TB Tuberculosis
UN United Nations
UNAIDS Joint UN Program on HIV/AIDS
UNDP United Nations Development Programme
UNGASS UN General Assembly Special Session on HIV/AIDS
UNICEF United Nations Children's Fund
USAID United States Agency for International Development
USDA United States Department of Agriculture
USG United States Government
WB World Bank
WHO World Health Organization

I. GHI Vision and Objectives

The US Government's (USG) vision for relations with Indonesia is the continued development of a broad and durable "Comprehensive Partnership" through which Indonesia, an emerging middle income country and developing regional and global power, and the US will work in partnership on priority goals and shared objectives. As stated in the US Embassy Jakarta mission statement, "Based on mutual respect and shared values, the US Mission works with Indonesia to strengthen democracy, sustain the environment, promote prosperity, enhance understanding, and ensure security for our people, our nations, and our region." Health activities undertaken by the whole of USG support Government of Indonesia (GOI) priorities and reflect the principles of this Comprehensive Partnership.

The USG vision for the Global Health Initiative (GHI) in Indonesia is to further strengthen the implementation, reach, and impact of health activities by increasing alignment, coordination and synergies across USG agencies in line with GOI priorities. Current activities and strategies throughout the USG health portfolio strongly reflect the core tenets of GHI – country ownership and whole of government approaches. The GHI goal for Indonesia is **"Improved Health Impact through Collaboration"** which will be achieved with concentrated efforts in three interrelated focus areas:

- *Catalyze action to accelerate Indonesia's progress toward achievement of Millennium Development Goals (MDG) 4, 5 and 6.* Achieving the MDGs is a very high priority for the GOI. There is recognition that aggressive action will be required to meet MDG 5 in particular.

> **MDGs targeted for focus:**
> - Goal 4: Reduce child mortality
> - Goal 5: Improve maternal health
> - Goal 6: Combat HIV/AIDS, malaria and other infectious diseases

- *Enhancing the use of quality research and evidence in policy and programming*, including introduction and adoption of new technologies and capacity building.
- *Partnering with the GOI to address regional and global infectious disease threats* and strengthen Indonesia's engagement and leadership in regional and global health issues and fora.

II. GHI in the Indonesian Context

Indonesia is the world's largest archipelago and fourth most populous country, consisting of about 240 million people from 300 ethnic groups, speaking 250 languages, scattered unevenly across about half of its 17,000 islands. Sixty percent of the population resides on the island of Java. The population is increasing at a greater rate than previously predicted, likely related to a de-emphasis of the national family planning (FP) programs and regional migration. Indonesia's vast size, government structure and diverse environment and cultures engender a unique health profile that includes regional variation in disease prevalence, mortality rates, health priorities, emergence of novel biological threats, and challenges in accessing quality health care. The country is administratively divided into 33 provinces and nearly 500 districts/ municipalities. Though guided by policies adopted at the national level, Indonesia is highly decentralized with decision-making authority and responsibility for action largely located at the district level.

GOI Priorities

The GOI's desire to achieve the MDGs is at the heart of its health programming. Health is identified as a priority for the GOI in the 2010-2014 National Medium-Term Development Plan. Additional strategies and plans from the Ministry of Health (MOH) and presidential decrees guide implementation of the plan. These include disease specific strategies, such as those for HIV/AIDS, tuberculosis (TB) control, immunization, lymphatic filariasis (LF) elimination, avian influenza (AI), and others focused on animal and human interactions. Presidential Decree No. 29/2011 succinctly describes several health priorities, harmonized with MOH budget allocations that are sufficiently cross-cutting to guide the GHI strategy:

- Prevention through integration of basic immunizations, providing access to quality water and sanitation to reduce maternal and infant mortality rates
- Revitalization of family planning by increasing quality and covering family planning services
- Improving health facilities by increasing number of internationally accredited hospitals
- Increased availability and accessibility of drugs .i.e., generics
- Universal health coverage for all Indonesia citizens

In relation to the GHI principle of 'women girls and gender equality,' the GOI is poised to be a strong partner. Presidential decree No. 9/2000 instructs all government bodies to implement gender mainstreaming for planning, formulation, implementation, monitoring and evaluation of national development policies and programs in accordance with their responsibilities, functions and authorities. This order has been followed by guidance for line ministries on its implementation.

USG footprint in Indonesia

The USG has had a long and successful history of work in the health sector in Indonesia. While USAID accounts for 94% of the USG budget in health for Indonesia, US Centers for Disease Control and Prevention (CDC), the National Institutes of Health (NIH), US Department of State Biosecurity Engagement Program (BEP), US Department of Agriculture (USDA) and Office of Defense Cooperation (DOD) also play significant roles, particularly in AI, other emerging pandemic threats (EPT) and HIV/AIDS in the case of DOD. The Peace Corps has recently returned to Indonesia after its departure in 1964 and is considering adding health to the sectors where Volunteers are active. The NIH is expected to enter into an expanded partnership and the Millennium Challenge Corporation (MCC), which previously provided support for childhood immunizations and is currently negotiating a new compact that includes a focus on reduction of stunting. As new USG agencies come to Indonesia, they will become part of the GHI Indonesia team.

The USG's long history and successful programming in Indonesia provides examples of the GHI principles in action. Working under the guidance of national strategies and priorities and in partnership with government and private sector, investing in innovation, putting the interests of women and girls at the center of programming and increasing impact through strategic coordination have all been core approaches used by the USG in Indonesia and will continue to guide its work. In this environment, the US has played a catalytic role, identifying key leverage points where specific, value-added support, typically technical input and cooperation, bring unique US strength and experience to address obstacles, unblock processes and quickly accelerate progress. US contributions have had significant impact:

- The USG was a key partner for Indonesia's successful FP program until its graduation from USG FP assistance in 2007. Contraceptive prevalence in Indonesia increased from less than 5% in the 1960s to over 60% in the late 1990s.
- USG-led approaches across the health sector, including maternal and child health (MCH), TB, HIV/AIDS and AI, have made the successful leap from project-based activities to replication and adoption by the GOI.
- USAID has seen success in involving men in support of early initiation of breast feeding and in developing emergency birth preparedness plans.
- Simple and cost-effective innovations which USAID has helped implement include kangaroo mother care for management of low birth weight babies, and roll-out of active management of third stage labor (AMTSL) and magnesium sulfate (MgSO4) for management of postpartum hemorrhage and eclampsia, respectively.

> ***Doing more of what works***
> *Desa Siaga,* or "Alert village," was introduced in the mid-1990s under a USAID program to ensure birth readiness and mutual support in responding to emergencies at the village level. The approach has been fully adopted by the GOI and integrated into other health programs requiring village level surveillance and action including avian influenza risk reduction.
>
> ***Moving from Pilot to Policy***
> The USAID-supported Participatory Disease Surveillance and Response system was adopted and integrated into the Indonesian National Veterinary Services.

- The USG has partnered with the National TB Program (NTP) over the past 10 years, helping the GOI meet global TB targets and begin the roll-out of MDR-TB diagnosis and treatment nationally.
- Working in partnership with UNICEF in Eastern Indonesia, the USG has successfully integrated malaria into antenatal care. In project districts using funding from several donors, malaria incidence declined by as much as 50% due to a combination of bed net use, screening and treatment, and community engagement.
- The USG has been a key partner in the implementation of the Global Fund to Fight AIDS, TB and Malaria (GFATM) grants in Indonesia. Indonesia is a major recipient of GFATM grants and the USG has made a significant contribution to successful proposal development, program implementation and development of tools and systems for more effective grant management and oversight.

With regard to the GHI principle of country ownership, the USG is exploring options of direct investment in host country systems in support of procurement and implementation reform. Additional concrete plans include providing a direct contribution to a fund for HIV managed by the National AIDS Commission, implementing the Global Fund dashboard to effectively monitor grants, direct assistance to Indonesian NGOs, small grants program in biosecurity, and fixed obligation grants to directly fund districts operating neglected tropical disease (NTD) control programs.

GHI Outcomes in Indonesia - where they stand and who is doing what

As the fourth largest country in the world, Indonesia's health status is of global significance. Its contribution to global health objectives, including GHI, is critical. Indonesia is the largest country that will have a GHI strategy, if Indonesia does not meet its MDGs and GHI targets, it will be difficult to meet global targets.

Achieving the MDGs is a high priority for the GOI. Achievement of the MDGs as well as the closely related GHI targets requires that the GOI and partners to address weaknesses in the quality of service delivery and of the healthcare system, as well as ensure accelerated action and engagement of a wide range of partners including the private sector and the science community.

Improving the skills of the clinical and public health workforces as well as the quality of care in the facilities where they work is essential to improving the health status of Indonesians. For this reason, much of the work supported by the USG cuts across the GHI targets, though often in the context of HIV, TB and MCH. In addition, at the heart of the GHI/Indonesia strategy is increased integration across all components of the portfolio. USG supports long-term degree training in public health and related fields, both in Indonesia and in the US, field epidemiology training and laboratory strengthening, and addresses quality of care in hospitals, including support for infection control in laboratories and facilities and ensuring implementation of international standards. Though much of the work supported by USAID is done through multilateral partners and large US-based implementers, Indonesian non-governmental organizations (NGO) and the GOI are increasingly direct implementing partners.

Other donors also work across the public health spectrum. AusAID has a substantial, broad health portfolio including programs in MCH, HIV/AIDS, pandemic influenza and health systems strengthening, which focuses on financing and human resources. AusAID and USAID work particularly closely and collaboratively to ensure effective coordination and complementarity of efforts. JICA has a broad health portfolio that complements the GHI, including programs in MCH, pandemic influenza, TB, rational drug use and vaccine production. Health systems approaches supported by JICA include installation and improvement of health facilities, improving university training and training for MCH providers and laboratory technicians. The UN and multi-laterals are also significant partners in the health sector. The USG works directly with the WHO, UNICEF, and FAO, and collaborates closely with UNAIDS as well as the World Bank and UNDP. These close collaborations cut across the portfolio, and efforts are coordinated in a thoughtful and strategic way. Effective donor collaboration is valued by the GOI, as such the USG engages regularly with international and multilateral donors in conjunction with the Ministry of Health International Cooperation Division as well as program area specific fora as with the CDC and WHO around immunization.

HIV/AIDS and TB: According to the 2009 Indonesia Country Report on the follow-up to the Declaration of Commitment on HIV/AIDS, the HIV epidemic in Indonesia is among the fastest growing in Asia. HIV infection rates are the highest in Papua (2.4%), where it has spread to the general population. With large mining, migrant worker and fishing industries, Papua is a likely source for increased HIV transmission throughout the region. In support of PEPFAR goals and GHI targets for prevention and treatment of HIV/AIDS, the USG supports the national HIV/AIDS strategy and action plan and focuses on building the capacity of local governments and NGOs to prevent HIV/AIDS among high-risk groups, increasing the effectiveness of GOI HIV/AIDS interventions and improving access to HIV/AIDS and other health services in Papua and West Papua. Under PEPFAR, DOD provides support for training, laboratory equipment and technical assistance to the Indonesian military in expanding HIV/AIDS prevention and services for personnel.

Indonesia has the fifth highest TB burden globally and ranks eighth for multi-drug resistant TB (MDR-TB). Although it is on track to achieve TB-related MDG targets, due to increased diagnosis, high prevalence and the global threat posed by TB and MDR-TB, the GOI and partners must continue to aggressively work to sustain current case detection rates and achieve global MDG and GHI targets. The USG provides technical assistance and training to the NTP to strengthen TB detection and case management, and facilitate early diagnosis and treatment. Diagnosis and treatment of MDR-TB in Indonesia began in 2010 with USAID support.

Indonesia has received GFATM grants since 2003 with 17 grants worth $500 million across the three diseases. Grants have been awarded to the MOH, National AIDS Commission and civil society partners. Grants to the MOH are used to procure all ARVs and many of the ACTs and MDR-TB treatment regimens in Indonesia. Programs strengthen and expand DOTS, train health workers, strengthen communications and community outreach, build the capacity of national, regional and provincial laboratories, improve quality and reach of service delivery, including opportunistic infections, TB/HIV coinfection, PMTCT, counseling and testing, enhance the health information system; support indoor residual spraying control and procurement of insecticide-treated nets, improve partner coordination, bridge the public and private sectors, and improve access to treatment for each of the diseases. The USG provides substantial, highly valued technical assistance (TA) to GFATM recipients in proposal development, implementation and management, and establishment of oversight systems. This TA is essential to program success. In addition, USG staff are members of the country coordinating mechanism (CCM) and technical working groups (TWG) and provide extensive TA to the CCM Secretariat.

Maternal and Child Health and Nutrition: Neonatal, infant and under-five mortality rates all decreased since the 1987 DHS, but have stagnated more recently (Table 1). Breastfeeding rates have been declining, and exclusive breastfeeding for the first six months decreased from 40% in 2002 to 32% in 2007. The leading causes of under-five mortality include: neonatal causes (38%), diarrheal diseases (18%), pneumonia (14%) and measles (5%) – all of which can improve with systems approaches such as training health workers on symptomatic diagnosis, expanding vaccination coverage and simplifying the referral process. Indonesia is considered on target for reducing child mortality in line with MDG 4, with sustained technical assistance from the USG and other donors.

Child nutritional status is a serious problem in Indonesia. Thirty-seven percent of children under five are stunted, with relatively high levels of acute malnutrition occurring among children particularly in the eastern islands. Indonesia is also beginning to see nutritional issues at the other extreme, with child obesity rates of 12%.

Table 1: Change for Mortality Ratios/Rates 1987-2007				
	1987	2007	% Change	MDG
Maternal Mortality Ratio	450/100,000	228/100,000	-49%	102/100,000
Neonatal mortality	27/1,000	19/1,000	-30%	Non-specific
Infant mortality	67/1,000	34/1,000	-49%	23/1,000
U5 mortality	100/1,000	44/1,000	-56%	32/1,000

Indonesia's maternal mortality is among the highest in the region, at an official ratio of 228/100,000. While this represents a decline from the ratio reported in previous years, it is far from the MDG target of 102/100,000 and an estimated 10,000 women die each year due to complications during labor and delivery. Most of these deaths are preventable. The leading causes of maternal mortality in Indonesia are hemorrhage (28%), eclampsia (24%), and sepsis (11%). Almost 50% of maternal deaths take place in health facilities, where poor quality of care and delayed referral are significant contributing factors. The GOI recognizes that much work still needs to be done in order to meet MDG 5. As a result, it has invested resources into community health centers and is paying special attention to use of antenatal care, skilled attendance at birth and availability of resources for emergency obstetric care.

USG programs focus directly on MCH, and therefore have a direct impact on Indonesia's ability to achieve GHI and MDG targets for maternal and child mortality. In support of the GOI national strategy for improving maternal and neonatal health, USAID strategically focuses on improving quality of maternal and newborn services, ensuring appropriate management of complications in facilities in accordance with internal standards, reducing delays within the emergency obstetrical care referral system, and improving governance and accountability. This focus on quality stems not from an assumption that improved quality will necessarily increase uptake of services, but rather from the realization that poor quality services currently contribute to mortality and morbidity. USAID supports oxygen therapy to treat ARIs, the second leading cause of death for children under five years. In addition, USAID supports the MOH to achieve its goal of dramatically increasing the number of hospitals that are internationally accredited. USAID mechanisms help civil society work with government to expand delivery and through oversight mechanisms improve the quality of care provided both at public and private health service facilities. The USG works with UNICEF to focus on improved access to high quality and comprehensive care during pregnancy, delivery and postnatal periods, including emergency referral and improving health information systems and knowledge exchange in Papua, West Papua, Maluku and North Maluku. Given the impact of malaria on maternal mortality in eastern Indonesia, this program also includes malaria in pregnancy interventions, fully integrated with the broader MCH services. It aims to improve access to bed nets for pregnant women, trains village midwives to deliver appropriate prevention and referral services and stimulates policy discussion with the MOH. In late 2011, the MCC is expected to sign a compact agreement with Indonesia that includes a component focused on the mitigation and prevention of stunting in children under two and pregnant women. This program will expand use of breastfeeding, use of appropriate complementary foods and micronutrient supplementation and improved sanitation.

Neglected Tropical Diseases and other infectious disease threats: Lymphatic filariasis (LF) and soil transmitted helminthaisis (STH) are endemic throughout Indonesia; Indonesia accounts for 9.3% of the world's at-risk population, with an estimated 125-200 million people at-risk for LF nationally. STH is a widespread problem affecting child health and development. In 2011, USAID began to provide critical support to the National LF Elimination Plan and national program for control of STH.

Indonesia is a hotspot for influenza and emerging diseases due to its biodiversity, climate, the close proximately of wildlife and livestock to humans and risky behaviors and practices which lead to disease dissemination. Indonesia is one of five countries still endemic for AI. The virus remains widespread across the massive poultry sector and continues to cause human illness and death. Indonesia has more AI cases than anywhere else in the world and the highest case fatality globally due to a weak disease surveillance system and delayed treatments. While there are no GHI targets specific to either AI or EPT, by building laboratory capacity to diagnose and monitor disease, improving diagnosis and care management of respiratory infections, expanding awareness among the population, strengthening the health care system and standards of care, training epidemiologists, and developing research skills, AI/EPT program outcomes impact maternal and child mortality, disease diagnostic capabilities and achievement of the GHI targets. USAID, CDC, USDA, and State Department through the Biosecurity Engagement Program (BEP), and DoD together help the MOH and GOI to strengthen laboratory systems, communication and community outreach, improve standards of care for patients and improved logistics and management of laboratory reagents and essential medicines. Work in AI improves management of respiratory infections, laboratories, hospital management and surveillance. This smart integration across USG agencies and program areas emphasizes improved disease control and treatment, and creates synergies across the USG health portfolio. Increased integration and synergy across the portfolio is an important outcome of the GHI strategy development process.

Other GHI Targets: At present, the USG does not directly support programs in FP and reproductive health or malaria. Indonesia graduated from USG FP assistance in 2007 when it had a contraceptive prevalence rate of 61.4% among married women and total fertility rate of 2.6. USAID, in its most recent MNCH project design, very carefully considered how to target limited MCH funding available to Indonesia to garner the largest impact. Therefore, in addition to management of complications, the MNCH project includes post-partum FP promotion in improved quality of care efforts. In addition, the USG encourages other donors (AusAID and the Gates Foundation) to expand investment into the existing gap of FP promotion, especially in regard to long lasting methods and method mix. Malaria is found throughout Indonesia and is endemic in eastern Indonesia with particularly high rates in Papua, Maluku and Nusa Tenggara. In these provinces, where people still lack basic preventive measures and receive poor diagnosis and inappropriate treatment and are highly mobile, malaria is a factor in increased risk for maternal and newborn morbidity and mortality. Although the USG health portfolio does not directly contribute to the GHI and MDG targets for these areas, cross-cutting efforts to improve the quality of care, disease surveillance and diagnosis, and underlying health status will have an indirect impact. Finally, USAID is partnering with UNICEF to support an integrated maternal child health and malaria in pregnancy effort in Papua, West Papua, and the Malukus.

Implementing the Women, Girls and Gender Equality Principle

Indonesia ranks 100th on the global Gender Equality Index. As with many social and health issues in Indonesia, gender, the role of women and girls and gender-based indicators are extraordinarily complex and vary widely across the country, and among different regional and ethnic groups. Socio-cultural environments range from the matrilineal societies in West Sumatra, where women are relatively empowered, to other regions and provinces where the rights of women and girls are severely compromised. Some disparities exist between Eastern Indonesia and other parts of Indonesia, stemming from ethnic differences; as such GHI programming pays special attention to underserved and disadvantage populations in these areas and Papua. In addition, transgendered individuals, or *waria*, are widely seen as a third gender and are particularly vulnerable to HIV/AIDS, social stigma and gender-based violence.

The most recent gender assessment was completed by the World Bank in 2008, the results of which are utilized in project design. In June 2011, a coalition of bilateral and multi-lateral agencies (CIDA, AusAID, World Bank, UKAID, and Asia Foundation) presented the GOI with a set of policy briefs detailing a series of findings and recommendations related to gender and programming within the development context. These policy briefs focused on, among others, gender mainstreaming, gender equity in health, women's voice in decision making, and violence against women. USG programming goals and activities are fully consistent with recommendations focused on maternal health, nutrition and HIV.

Attention to gender-based barriers to health services and gender-driven vulnerabilities is fully imbedded in the GHI Indonesia programs and strategy. Maternal survival and the health of women and girls are at the heart of the GHI Indonesia strategy. For example, maternal health programs address gender-based barriers to services, such as eliminating practices or policies that require a woman's husband consent before she is referred for emergency obstetrical care. The MCC-funded stunting program will also include a focus on reducing poor nutrition among pregnant women. HIV/AIDS activities pay particular attention to gender and are focused on prevention among most at-risk populations – many of whom are at risk because of gender or women's empowerment issues, including female sex workers and *waria*. Across the portfolio, GHI Indonesia will build on gender-related lessons learned in the past (*Desa Siaga*, *Program Perencanaan Persalinandan Pencegahan Komplikasi* P4K, and kangaroo mother care which were particularly concerned with gender barriers to services) as well as continue to collect gender disaggregated data and encourage policy-makers and community decision-makers to be aware of and proactively address the needs of women and girls in society. In research and science partnerships, GHI Indonesia will also encourage expanded participation of women scientists.

III. Focus Areas

The USG in Indonesia has been ahead of the curve in applying the whole of government approach and embracing country ownership. Like many USG Missions in Asia, health programs are predominantly implemented by USAID and other USG agencies co-locate in USAID, host government, or international partner offices. The health profile of Indonesia is also unique - HIV prevalence is low but rising, TB, MDR-TB, and other infectious disease threats are highly significant and approaches to tackle them are on the cutting edge. An abundance of life-saving, evidenced-based approaches in MCH are ready to be taken to scale and addressed systematically. Indonesia's unique geography and decentralization also require unique approaches. The Indonesia GHI strategy is designed to have a significant impact on several of the GHI targets:

- A 25% additional reduction in national maternal mortality and neonatal mortality
- Contribute to the treatment of 1,000,000 additional TB patients and the diagnosis and treatment of 5,100 MDR-TB patients over the next five years

- For NTDs, reduce prevalence of LF by 50% in 70% of the affected population as part of the national LF elimination plan and treat 100 million people each year for soil transmitted helminthaisis
- In HIV/AIDS reach 70% of most at risk groups with priority prevention interventions[1]
- In nutrition through the MCC, contribute to a significant reduction in stunting among young children and pregnant women

The GHI strategy also gives the USG Indonesia team the opportunity to build great efficiencies and connections both among program elements specifically focused on GHI targets as well as related USG supported programs such as avian and pandemic influenza.

The focus areas for GHI Indonesia are designed to ensure maximum impact on targets, build greater connections and effectiveness among the program components and leverage great engagement of the science community. Encouraging innovations, including use of new technologies and approaches, and exploiting information and communication technology to the greatest extent possible is embedded throughout the GHI Indonesia strategy, and within the Indonesian context, critical to the success of the health objectives in Indonesia.

The focus areas themselves are interconnected. Acceleration of Indonesian progress towards reaching MDGs 4, 5, and 6 is fueled by a greater capacity to collect and use data and research in implementation of disease and mortality fighting programs, which are strengthened by attention to quality through application of international standards. Engaging Indonesia more extensively in international fora will improve implementation of programs, help ensure implementation

> *Immunization: working across the focus areas*
> Measles continues to be an important cause of under-five mortality in Indonesia, with an estimated 20,000 cases annually, despite a reported measles vaccine coverage of over 90% and a national Measles elimination strategy that supplements routine immunization with campaigns. In response to this, a recent review of Indonesia's measles immunization program was done, including participation from the CDC. The review noted that the current immunization schedule is not in line with international standards, and leaves children in the one to nine year old age group particularly vulnerable. It also found that the reported coverage was lower than that found in surveys, providing an inaccurate view of program performance. Under the GHI strategy, the USG through CDC will provide targeted and long term technical assistance to improve the immunization schedule and implementation of the immunization program (FA 1), and support encourage Ministry of Health counterparts to improve the quality and use data on mortality and coverage to better monitor program implementation and improve coverage strategies (FA 2). The USG will also look for opportunities to engage GOI counterparts in international immunization and measles fora (FA 3) to encourage adoption of international standards and practices and accelerate implementation.

of international standards, and contribute to achievement of GHI targets, like those for NTDs, TB and immunization. The strategy also includes an emphasis on systems strengthening that mirrors the GOI's own strategies and will allow the USG to leverage existing resources while at the same time contribute substantially to changes in quality of care in all areas of public health and clinical care, which will not stop at the GHI targets, but see a life beyond 2015.

---

[1] This target is contingent upon a sustained HIV fund level consistent with FY 11; reduced funding will result in a smaller population reached.

Focus Area 1: Catalyze action to accelerate Indonesia's progress toward achievement of MDGs 4, 5 and 6

Over the past 25 years, there have been substantial improvements in basic health and social indicators in Indonesia, but there is still much to be done to achieve its health-related MDGs (See Annex One). Indonesia's achievements carry significant weight in the global achievement of MDG and GHI targets. In its recent review of progress against MDGs, the GOI identified the need to strengthen health systems, improve access to health services, expand better quality health care and involve all stakeholders – all of which are reflected in this strategy.[2] Through the GHI implementation, USG agencies will work together on three cross-cutting leverage points that complement and support GOI strategies and catalyze actions and progress toward the MDGs. These leverage points form the Intermediate Results (IR) for accelerating progress outlined below. In all cases, USG agencies will work together on these common priorities, building on current activities, introducing innovation, increasing coordination and accelerating the rate of program learning across the portfolio – working together and with partners to solve problems and achieve impact as quickly as possible.

Results in Focus Area (FA) 1 will be achieved by supporting achievement in three critical and mutually-dependent cross-cutting areas. Through IR 1.1, "Improved quality and effectiveness of government and private health systems", both supply and demand for life-saving, evidence-based interventions to reduce mortality from maternal, neonatal and infectious disease causes will be strengthened. Quality of facility-based care, laboratory strengthening, and improved disease recognition and referral systems are common needs in all areas and will be addressed. The long-term, large-scale effectiveness of these IR 1.1 supported interventions will be achieved by catalyzing the development of a supportive enabling environment at the district level (IR 1.2) and leveraging successful approaches and district programs to large scale implementation through district to district, regional and national mechanisms (IR 1.3).

IR 1.1: Improved quality and effectiveness of government and private health systems

The Indonesian health care system is a mix of private and public providers. There is significant overlap between the two systems because the GOI allows public sector clinicians to engage in private practice. Indonesians seek care in both systems and recent surveys show that use of the private sector is increasing, even among the poor. To date there are not systems and practices in place to ensure that providers comply with the accepted minimum clinical standards of care, leading to poor quality of care in both sectors and at all levels. The lack of systems to properly govern the public and private health sectors and resulting poor quality of care impedes progress on MDG and GHI targets for MCH and Infectious Disease. The USG Mission uses a whole-of-government approach to improve health service delivery. In addition to direct assistance to Ministry of Health hospitals, State is working with the Ministry of Health and others in the GOI to lift non-tariff barriers to trade in health service delivery, pharmaceutical imports, and importation of re-manufactured equipment

Through the GHI, USG agencies will improve governance of the healthcare system and the quality of healthcare services. Quality of care and compliance with standards at primary care facilities and

---

[2] *Source: Ministry of National Development Planning, Report on the achievement of the Millennium Development Goals Indonesia, 2010*

hospitals will be improved in districts in five high-priority provinces, with a focus on responding to maternal and newborn complications. Quality of care at hospitals will also improve through a three-way partnership to establish hospital accreditation between USAID, the MOH and WHO. Expanded referral systems for pregnant and delivering women and newborns will ensure that women and their babies receive timely, life-saving care. ICT and social media tools will be used to improve referrals and quality of care by engaging civil society and increasing accountability. Indonesia is number two in the world for use of Facebook and other social media and by the end of 2011, 95% of Indonesian households are expected to have access to a mobile phone. Laboratory strengthening will be supported to improve the accuracy and appropriateness of diagnosis and treatment for TB, MDR-TB, HIV, and viruses including AI. Health care providers, community health workers and policy makers will be better able to recognize and respond to illness as USG assistance strengthens early warning systems for respiratory outbreaks and provide training on syndromic surveillance. The EPT program will expand beyond syndromic surveillance to develop and use predictive models (based on research and molecular biology) to try to forecast emerging diseases. As the quality of care is improved, the population will increasingly expect better quality services, creating a productive dynamic between supply and demand.

IR 1.2: District capacity, leadership and health governance improved in a decentralized, district-led system

In the late 1990s Indonesia underwent dramatic and rapid decentralization. While central authorities continue to have influence, district leaders and local parliaments retain a significant amount of decision-making authority on allocations for health and other programs. Sustaining the improvements in quality of care needed to meet the MDGs requires district-level investment, commitment and the capacity to govern. Improving priority-setting for health requires on-going advocacy at the district level and building the capacity of district authorities to take on a greater oversight and regulatory role. A number of district authorities are open to implementing progressive and dynamic public health policies and programs, and their stories of success are used to gain influence for work in new districts. Work at the district level expands opportunities to involve women in decision-making and governance at the local and district levels.

Applying the GHI principle of country ownership, investing in successful implementation of decentralized programming is key to achieving the MDGs in Indonesia. Under the GHI, USG will improve district leadership to plan and implement effective, evidence-based health programs, maternal and child interventions including disease surveillance and mass drug administration programs. District management and oversight of health services will be improved, including development of sufficient health budgets and improved transparency and accountability including engagement of civil society. USG efforts will also help the GOI to respond to increased demand for responsive district health program priorities.

IR 1.3: High impact health interventions effectively implemented at scale in Indonesia

In order to accelerate national-level progress toward achieving MDGs 4, 5 and 6, not only must evidence-based, effective district-led health services be implemented with high quality, but these efforts must be brought to regional and in some cases national scale. USG will work with partners to leverage and expand successful district programs province-wide. Effective, high priority, evidence-based interventions will be integrated into the health system, such as scale up of the international standards of care for TB, kangaroo mother care for newborns and scale up of zinc supplementation for diarrhea. USAID and CDC will continue to partner with UNICEF in eastern Indonesia to integrate MCH with malaria programs; ensuring that vulnerable women and children have access to prevention tools throughout Papua. At the national level, USG will coordinate with multi and bi-lateral partners to achieve synergies in support of wide-scale impact to achieve the MDGs, building on efforts that have brought USAID, CDC, the MOH and WHO together for AI to improve management of acute respiratory infections (ARI). The impact of health sector programs will be increased and expanded through strategic cross-sectoral coordination and integration, largely in the area of EPT, where the USG works with the Ministry of Agriculture on animal surveillance and outbreak response and with the private sector to improving cleaning and disinfection throughout the poultry supply chain. Further work will engage and leverage the private sector to support large scale health objectives, such as working with the NTP to build linkages with private sector hospitals to scale up TB and MDR-TB diagnosis and treatment.

Focus Area 2: Enhancing the Use of Quality Research and Evidence in Policy and Programming

Scientific research, technology and innovation are essential to solving today's most pressing development issues and are critical drivers of economic growth around the globe. Limitations in the use of data for policies and program implementation also impede progress. Indonesia, with the health and disease landscape described above, is a crucial partner to foster innovative development solutions which will have a broad impact globally, exemplified by its early adoption of *Xpert* technology and the Hain test for MDR- and TB diagnosis. However, like most developing countries, Indonesia is not a leader in scientific research and technology developments. A study by Harvard concluded that Indonesia's weak science sector has been a major impediment for its long-term development potential.[3] Some key issues which have been identified for Indonesia are poor quality and availability of data, lack of evidence-based decision making, limited use of technology and innovation, inadequately trained workforce and lack of coordination across sectors - particularly limited involvement of university scientists and the private sector.

Partnerships in science and technology are a high priority to the USG overall in Indonesia, not only in health. The GHI objectives related to science and research are fully embedded in and part of a much larger USG effort to expand Science and Technology (S&T) partnerships in Indonesia. Indonesia stands to make large gains through the bilateral S&T agreement with the US which will broaden and expand relations between the scientific communities of both countries across all fields of science, importantly public health. The White House Science Envoy for Indonesia, Dr. Bruce Alberts, is bringing fruition to President Obama's "New Beginning" vision of S&T engagement with the Muslim world through his work. Dr. Alberts has met with the Indonesian President, Ministers, Academies of Science, and numerous universities to advance cooperation in scientific research, education, innovation, business development, and health. This S&T partnership is an important component of the Comprehensive Partnership and

---

[3] From Reformasi to Institutional Transformation: A Strategic Assessment of Indonesia's Prospects for Growth, Equity, and Democratic Governance, Harvard Kennedy School Indonesia Program.

priorities areas include: strengthening and improving the overall capacity for science and math education; increasing multi-discipline research capacity based on competitive peer reviewed practices; fostering enabling environments for innovation; facilitating academic exchanges, training opportunities, and sustained collaborations; providing assistance to incorporate science and technology into evidence based decision making; and meeting the MDGs. Science, technology, and innovation efforts in other program sectors including, education, environment, and economic growth, will contribute to the goals outlined in this Focus Area.

Reinforcing the S&T agreement and addressing the critical issues identified, Focus Area 2 encompasses a range of efforts to improve the use of data resulting from basic, applied, translational, and operational research; and quantitative and qualitative studies and surveys.[4] Activities aim to enhance coordination beyond the health sector and increase regional and international collaborations. An important part of this focus area is the ability to assist Indonesia to better utilize quality data to improve public health policies and programming, essential to making progress towards GHI targets. Recently, AusAID conducted an assessment of the knowledge sector which revealed weakness in policy development because of limited evidence used in decision making.[5] Due to a weak education system and health care training, much of the workforce is ill-equipped to adequately or robustly analyze data. Additionally, a lack of coordination across divisions within the MOH, and other Ministries, leads to ineffective use of data.

To achieve this goal, more efforts are needed to enhance workforce capacity, improve tools and systems and strengthen policies on data use. Capacity building is needed at several levels to accomplish this, encompassing pre-service education, work force training, infrastructure improvement, creating an enabling environment to introduce new technologies, and changes in policies and practices to achieve quality standards and to disseminate and use evidence in decision making. The USG presently supports training efforts for professionals and university students, provides assistance to analyze the Demographic Health Survey (DHS) data and makes data more accessible to users through publication of results such as the IBBS data. Under GHI, the USG will continue to increase human resources capacity for evidence-based decision making through training and assistance to develop evidence based strategies and policies/regulations. It will support linkages between the traditional public health sector, policy makers and scientists and researchers, including the development of health-related policy reports by Indonesian institutions. USG will assist partners in translating data into public health actions at the policy and service delivery levels. For example, USAID is supporting a stigma and discrimination survey aimed at health personnel in HIV intervention sites that are identified by most at-risk populations as the health facilities they visit. Survey results will be used to develop standard operational procedures for service providers for most-at-risk populations. Operational Research (OR) assessments of USG-funded activities will provide a feedback loop that uses lessons learned to improve approaches to project

---

[4] Research can be defined as the search for knowledge through systematic investigation or scientific method to establish new facts, solve problems, prove new ideas, or develop new theories. The primary purpose for basic research is discovering, interpreting, and developing methods and systems for the advancement of knowledge. Operational research provides decision-makers with information to enable them to improve the performance of their programs, i.e. to identify solutions to problems that limit program quality, efficiency and effectiveness.

[5] Report is not yet published; findings were presented at a Knowledge Sector Meeting in Jakarta on June 15, 2011.

implementation. The USG's role on the GFATM Country Coordinating Mechanism (CCM) will ensure that the information provided in the GFATM Dashboard, just rolling-out in Indonesia, is utilized to improve oversight of the GFATM grants and ultimately improve the grant performance, critically important to achieving the national MDG and GHI targets.

Overall, FA 2 will improve the use of quality research in Indonesia, improve the availability and "offer" of new interventions and innovations to include in health efforts, and increase the availability and access to data and information for program monitoring and improvement. FA 2 emphasizes capacity building throughout, and supports the other two FAs by providing the means to answer priority questions and provide critical information and new tools to enable the achievements of FA1 and FA3, as well as those more generally in the health sector in Indonesia. Specifically, dialogue with stakeholders and identification of key questions where answers are needed to accelerate program impact under FA1 and FA3 will provide the "front end" for FA2 activities, which will assure provision of essential information, the capacity and productivity to conduct quality research, and a supply of new interventions and innovations where possible - all to meet the needs of health programs and for health policy formulation.

IR 2.1: Improved availability of good quality data for programming and policies to improve public health

While there are many systems in place to generate and collect data in Indonesia, there are still gaps, suspect quality and lack of external quality assurance, and poor dissemination from district to province to central level. USG support is provided for improved use of data at the local and central levels across the portfolio (including MCH, HIV/AIDS, TB, AI and NTDs); from USAID support for the Indonesia Demographic Health Survey (IDHS) that generates the most accurate population-based health status data every five years to CDC and USAID support for an animal and human influenza surveillance system. Under the GHI, USG will continue to help the GOI improve its disease surveillance, expanding the network to encompass a broader range of febrile illness and other emerging diseases. Supply chain tracking systems have been installed and through a university partnership an integrated health data repository will be established. There is an increasing focus on understanding and surveying health behavior – particularly in the HIV, TB, and ARI efforts. Public health behavior surveys and studies, such as the Integrated Biological Behavior Surveillance (IBBS) for HIV in Papua and operational research (OR) to understand barriers for condom use will also be supported. Data collection and tracking systems will be strengthened through scaling-up of systems like e-TB manager, which tracks MDR-TB treatment and drug supplies.

IR 2.2: New technologies and innovations introduced to impact public health outcomes

Health outcomes can greatly improve with effective and appropriate use of technology and innovations. Technologies can improve the speed and accuracy of diagnosis, which leads to faster and appropriate treatments. Examples in Indonesia include support for the AMTSL and use of magnesium sulfate for management of post-partum hemorrhaging and eclampsia, respectively, or using zinc supplements to prevent childhood diarrhea. Sophisticated technologies, introducing technologies such as *Xpert* and Hain test, for more accurate and rapid MDR-TB and TB/HIV testing and rapid testing for malaria, which is being done at the village level, are additional examples of the public health impact technologies and innovations are having in Indonesia.

Technology can also be a tool to increase demand for quality services. Innovative use of mobile phones continues to evolve and improve communications, helping providers and individuals to access information to better recognize symptoms and understand diagnosis and treatment as well as better behaviors for prevention. Use of communication technologies will be a key to component of maternal health programs. They will give providers a tool for making prompt and appropriate referrals. Other innovation enhances advocacy, such as introduction of the computer-based Resource Estimate Tools for Advocacy, which provides local leaders with estimates of the resources needed for a five-year period, based on user input of population size estimates, target coverage levels, and local costs of HIV prevention services.

New methodologies and tools will need to be developed to detect emerging diseases. The USG will continue to support existing technologies and encourage new innovation under GHI. A Clinical Research Network is being established which will create local capacity to develop and test new medical products. New scientific methodologies have been introduced which support the GOI to track the influenza antigen shift develop new innovative vaccines, and to promote their rational use. GHI will facilitate public-private partnerships to increase innovation and research and development.

IR 2.3: Expanded and Improved Quality Health Research
Both USAID and HHS, through NIH and CDC, are growing their Indonesia portfolios in health research in response to increased opportunities for partnership with the MOH. Recent progress at the World Health Assembly regarding sample sharing through the resolution on Pandemic Influenza Preparedness will yield increased transparency of data and efforts and active participation in the international forum for diseases should result in improved research partnerships between the USG and GOI. Efforts currently underway include: a) tracking the influenza virus to develop new poultry vaccines; b) funding for a TB Operational Research Group which has expanded clinical case management for TB and MDR-TB; c) a joint Science Academy program *Frontiers in Science* which includes a focus on the biogeography of infectious diseases and; d) establishing university collaborations.

International partnerships will increase basic and applied research in the public health field and improve the standards and quality of the research that is conducted. USAID supports the Partnerships for Enhanced Engagement in Research program, a mechanism which facilitates scientific partnerships and funds competitively awarded research grants; a joint National Academy of Science's report on reduction of maternal and neonatal mortality rates; and CDC (with UNICEF) is reviewing the quality of the measles vaccination program. HHS will place a scientist at the MOH's National Institute for Health Research and Development (NIHRD) and NIAID is implementing a Clinical Research Network.

Focus Area 3: Partnering to address regional and global infectious disease threats
Indonesia must be able to respond effectively to endemic and emerging infectious diseases, including vaccine-preventable diseases, and protect the health of its citizens. With the fifth highest TB burden, the highest incidence of AI globally, 10% of the world's LF at-risk population, relatively high rates of measles death, and natural tropical climate, infectious diseases will continue to have national and global implications. Indonesia is also poised to take a regional and even global leadership role in prevention

and response to infectious disease threats, especially those relevant to the GHI (TB, NTDs, and HIV). Its leadership potential, through its convening capacity and political weight via its membership in the G-20 and leadership in ASEAN, its relations with other Muslim countries and its positive relationship with the West and global multilaterals, can serve as a model for and greatly improve global preparedness and response against infectious diseases of global and regional significance. In addition, increased engagement in regional and global technical groups and consultations can help improve policy and program implementation in Indonesia.

Focus Area 3 aims to support and strengthen Indonesia's position as a regional and global leader in disease threat management and response, and to encourage the use of international standards for disease care treatment (TB, NTD, MCH, HIV) by increasing engagement of key decision makers in international health forums. FA3 will support GOI abilities to monitor and address emerging disease threats within Indonesia (IR 3.1), to provide leadership regionally and globally on matters of infectious disease control (IR 3.2), and thereby strengthen Indonesia's ability to achieve international standards of care.

IR 3.1: Improved preparedness and ability to respond to global and regional infectious disease threats

USG in Indonesia supports improved implementation of infectious disease programs of global and regional significance in accordance with international disease control standards. USG assistance is at the cutting edge - developing and testing model approaches and technologies that show promise for regional and global replication to improve diagnosis, treatment and surveillance of infectious disease threats. For example, the USG supports strategies to ensure effective diagnosis and treatment of MDR-TB through its Programmatic Management Drug Treatment (PMDT) program, which focuses on the global threat of MDR- and XDR-TB. Indonesia will be one of three countries globally to introduce and test the new diagnostic technology *Xpert*, which promises to reduce the time required to diagnose MDR-TB and associated delays in appropriate treatment. Similarly, Indonesia is one of few countries that could develop the capacity to produce high-quality pharmaceuticals. The USG is providing technical assistance to local pharmaceutical manufacturers to obtain WHO pre-qualification for producing TB drugs to help address the global shortage of these essential medicines. Indonesia will host the regional TEPHINET meeting, which combine both scientific sessions and workshops related to managing public health systems and training programs, with assistance from USAID and CDC.

Significant investments are being made by CDC and USAID to improve the diagnostic capacity of laboratory facilities and build local capacity for TB, NTD and other disease control. The investments for disease-specific interventions contribute to and reinforce the general capacity of the country to diagnose, map and monitor disease prevalence and treatment success for all infectious diseases. Under the GHI, these disease specific efforts will be closely coordinated. BEP supports laboratory capacity building which is needed for infectious disease research in Indonesia. Working in collaboration with MOH and coordinated with the GFATM, USAID has renovated TB laboratories to meet international standards. Through GHI, laboratory capacity will be enhanced with facility renovations, training and introduction of new methodologies and technologies.

Increased commitment to and leadership in global health priorities

USG investments engage Indonesian health leaders in high-level global dialogue on strategic initiatives and policy development as a means of motivating Indonesian policy-makers to commit to and assure high quality control programs through engagement with their technical peers. For example, a senior MOH director is a member (the only female member) of the Board of Directors of the Global Alliance for the Elimination of LF, which leverages Indonesia's leadership and commitment to eliminating NTDs and adherence with global standards for disease control.

IV. Communications and Management Plan

Engaging stakeholders: The GHI Indonesia team uses a broad and comprehensive approach for communicating with and engaging the GOI, civil society and other partners, including international partners active in Indonesia. Collaboration between the USG and GOI historically and under the Indonesia GHI strategy promotes country ownership, as the USG participates in and supports existing mechanisms rather than creating its own committees, and is closely coordinated with GOI priorities and counterparts, including officials from the relevant Ministries and directorates within Ministries including: the MOH, the Coordinating Ministry for People's Welfare, the National HIV/AIDS Commission, the Ministry of Agriculture and the Indonesian Military through DOD. On specific activities such as support for the 2012 Demographic and Health Survey, the USG team also works closely with the Family Planning Coordinating Board (BKKBN). In addition, USG staff and partners also communicate and partner closely with counterparts at the district, municipality and provincial levels. This engagement and communication approach uses both regular formal meeting and agreement structures and informal means of communication at different levels. Formal structures include:

- Quarterly bilateral meetings between the MOH and the US Embassy Health team, co-chaired by the Secretary General of the Ministry of Health and the US Deputy Chief of Mission
- Participation and formal membership in Indonesian commissions and formal coordinating structures such as:
  - Representation on the Indonesian Country Coordination Mechanism for the GFATM (this includes extensive engagement with GOI and civil society partners);
  - Participation in the KOMNAS (National Committee) Zoonosis;
  - USAID membership in the Indonesia Partnership Fund Steering Committee for HIV/AIDS, represented by the USAID Mission Director;
  - Membership in the Global Alliance for Vaccines and Immunization health systems strengthening and partner working group; and
  - USAID's membership in the Stop TB Partnership Forum Indonesia.
- USAID's programs fall under a formal bilateral agreement signed with the Coordinating Ministry for People's Welfare. Discussions are underway to develop a more detailed implementation plan with the MOH.
- Research efforts fall under the formal S&T agreement recently signed by the GOI and USG. HHS and NIH are currently in discussion regarding appropriate arrangements for engagement in Indonesia.

- Later in 2011, a formal MCC Compact agreement is expected to be signed by the USG and the GOI.[6]

USG internal communication and management processes: All USG agencies working in health meet monthly in the Health Sector Working Group (HSWG). Organized by the Embassy and formally chaired by the Deputy Chief of Mission, these routine meetings are a forum for sharing information, and updating one another on recent developments or upcoming activities of general interest. Members of the HSWG include: State Department, CDC, USAID, DOD, USDA and the Embassy Medical Unit. In addition to the formal HSWG structure, members of the USG Indonesia health team indeed work together as a single team. Productive, consultative relationships are well established, information and updates are regularly shared and there is on-going and regular communication. There is a high degree of trust and comfort in the HSWG relationship, such that any one agency representative is empowered to speak for the whole USG health team. Additionally, various USG agencies are members of specific teams (such as USAID and CDC on malaria in pregnancy and MCH; CDC, USAID and USDA on AI; and USAID and DOD on HIV/AIDS) and meet regularly and share information and program updates. In addition to the formal structures, members of the interagency health sector working group communicate almost on a daily basis to strategize, update on progress, and report on meetings at the Ministry of Health. Because of the productive nature of the formal and informal interagency group, HSWG members often represent other agencies interests in meetings at the Ministry of Health.

> **_Applying the Whole of Government Principle_**
> This past year, the Indonesia HSWG worked together to successfully establish a new health objective under the Mission Strategic and Resource Plan. This objective reflects the strategy and components of the GHI strategy and is the product and responsibility of the full USG health team in Indonesia working together.

The GHI strategy development has allowed the Indonesia team to accelerate efficiencies within the program and integration across the portfolio. While the Indonesia team also had excellent interagency collaboration, coordination and relationships, the development of the FGHI strategy deepened these relationships even further.

Monitoring and Evaluation: The accompanying Results Framework and Matrix of activities for this GHI Strategy can be found in the annex.

---

[6] Specific MCC participation in focus areas and their contribution to GHI targets will be elaborated as this collaboration is finalized.

Annex One: Indonesia's Indicator Table

GHI Indicator Title (BY FOCUS AREA)	GHI Baseline	GHI Target
Reduction in maternal mortality	228/100,000	102/100,000
Reduction in neonatal mortality	19/1,000	15/1,000
Focus Area 1: Catalyze action to accelerate Indonesia's progress toward achievement of MDGs 4, 5 and 6		
Number of MDR- TB patients diagnosed and treated*	15,300 (2010 cases)	5,100 in FY14
Number of key population reached with HIV prevention interventions*	48,355 in FY11	84,390 in FY12
1.1.1 Number of hospitals accredited	3	25
1.1.2 Percentage of hospitals compliant with standard operating practices and/or minimum standards of care*	10	50%
1.1.3 Number of laboratories with improved diagnostics	5	17
1.1.4 Percentage of laboratories doing cross-check for QA	25 in FY10	50 in FY12
1.1.5 Percentage of laboratories meeting EQA standards for drug susceptibility	5 in FY10	9 in FY12
1.2.1 Number of districts budgeting at least 25% for health programs*	0	TBD
1.2.2 Number of districts engaging civil society in health system oversight*	TBD	TBD
1.3.1 Number of PMDT sites operating at scale	2	10
1.3.2 Percentage of women receiving AMTSL*	TBD	50%
Focus Area 2: Enhancing the Use of Quality Research and Evidence in Policy and Programming		
Measles vaccination program is re-designed to meet international standards	No	Yes
New evidence based policies developed pertaining to improving and monitoring drug quality and management	0	2
Neglected Tropical Disease (NTD) implementations strategies are developed or revised based on recent data	No	Yes
Case management policies are developed for XDR in line with WHO guidance	No	Yes
2.1.1 Increased citations and publications from the Indonesia Demographic Health Survey (IDHS) results	TBD	50
2.1.2 Quality disease surveillance data is made available through increased number of reputable public scientific databases, public health websites , and relevant dashboards	3	6
2.2.1 New technologies and innovation reaching 25 % of targeted population*	0	5
2.2.2 Relevant WHO priority policies and approaches are adopted after 1 year after recommended and endorsed	N/A	1
2.2.3 Private and public partnership established to enhance research and development	TBD	TBD

2.3.1 Number of peer-reviewed health publications increase at selected research partner institutes	0	9
2.3.2 Science Citation rates and the journal impact factor for health related publications improved at selected research institutes	TBD	10
2.3.3 Number of internationally accreditations increased (ISO certification, biosafety, IRBs)	5	17
Focus Area 3: Partnering to address regional and global infectious disease threats		
# of programs supported by USG in full compliance with international standards	1	4
3.1.1 Percentage of laboratories doing cross-check for QA	25 in FY10	50 in FY12
3.1.2 Percentage of laboratories meeting EQA standards for drug susceptibility	5 in FY10	9 in FY12
3.1.3 Number of drug companies receiving WHO pre-qualification	0	5 (1st and 2nd line)
3.2.1 # of international forums in which Indonesian MOH officials participate	2	5

* indicates in USG targeted areas only

Science Citation Index Expanded is a multidisciplinary index to the journal literature of the sciences. It fully indexes over 6,650 major journals across 150 scientific disciplines and includes all cited references captured from indexed articles. The SCI expanded database allows a researcher to identify which later articles have cited any particular earlier article, or cited the articles of any particular author, or determine which articles have been cited most frequently; some field have their own citation indexes.

Impact factor is a measure reflecting the average number of citations to articles published in science and social science journals. It is frequently used as a proxy for the relative importance of a journal within its field, with journals with higher impact factors deemed to be more important than those with lower ones. Journal impact factors are published annually in SCI Journal Citation Reports. A list is impact factors for specific journals can be found at: http://www.sciencegateway.org/rank/index.html

Annex Two: Indonesia GHI Results Framework

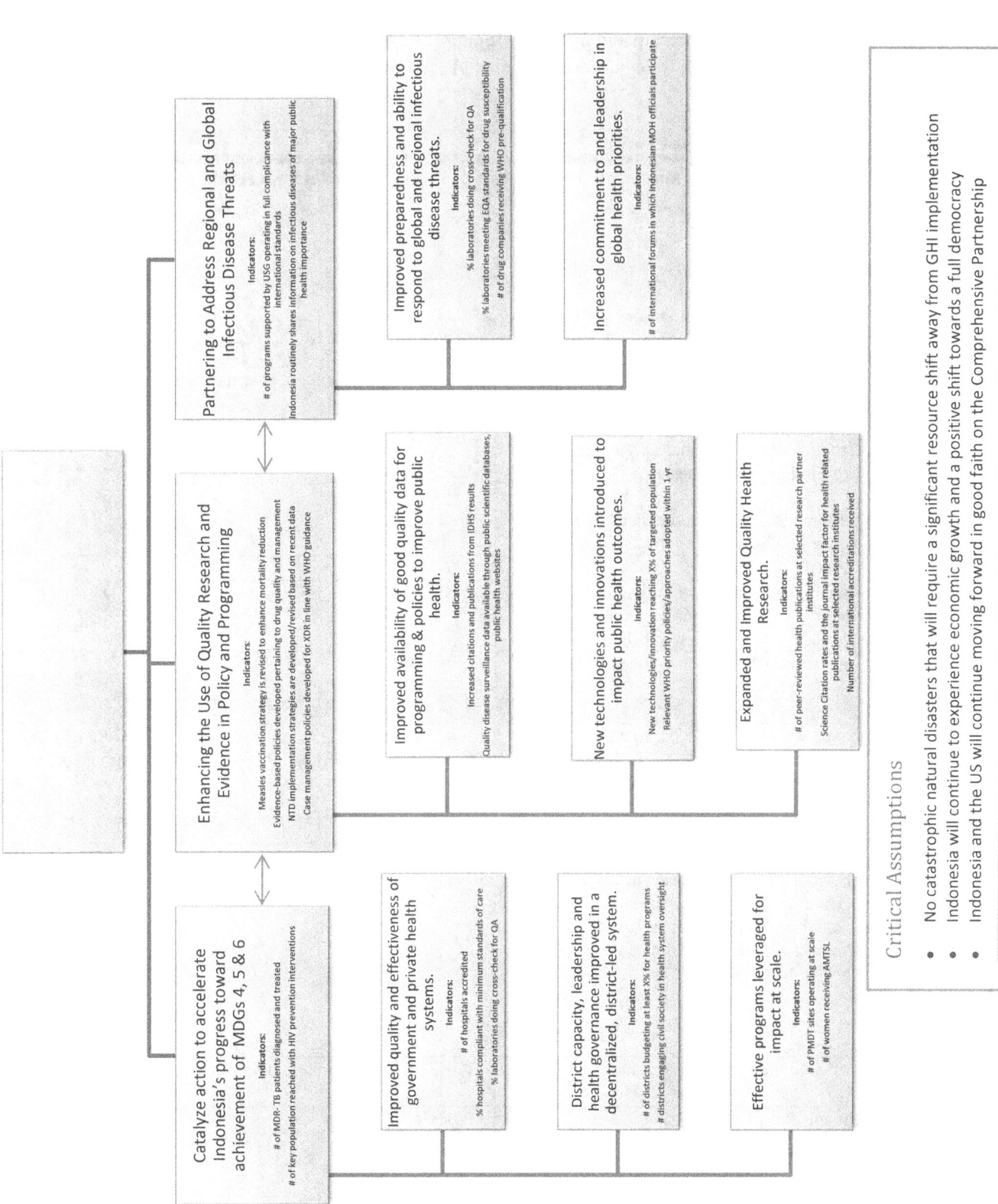

Catalyze action to accelerate Indonesia's progress toward achievement of MDGs 4, 5 & 6

Indicators:
# of MDR- TB patients diagnosed and treated
# of key population reached with HIV prevention interventions

Enhancing the Use of Quality Research and Evidence in Policy and Programming

Indicators:
Measles vaccination strategy is revised to enhance mortality reduction
Evidence-based policies developed pertaining to drug quality and management
NTD implementation strategies are developed/revised based on recent data
Case management policies developed for XDR in line with WHO guidance

Partnering to Address Regional and Global Infectious Disease Threats

Indicators:
# of programs supported by USG operating in full compliance with international standards
Indonesia routinely shares information on infectious diseases of major public health importance

Improved preparedness and ability to respond to global and regional infectious disease threats.

Indicators:
% laboratories doing cross-check for QA
% laboratories meeting EQA standards for drug susceptibility
# of drug companies receiving WHO pre-qualification

Increased commitment to and leadership in global health priorities.

Indicators:
# of international forums in which Indonesian MOH officials participate

Improved availability of good quality data for programming & policies to improve public health.

Indicators:
Increased citations and publications from IDHS results
Quality disease surveillance data available through public scientific databases, public health websites

New technologies and innovations introduced to impact public health outcomes.

Indicators:
New technologies/innovation reaching X% of targeted population
Relevant WHO priority policies/approaches adopted within 1 yr

Expanded and Improved Quality Health Research.

Indicators:
# of peer-reviewed health publications at selected research partner institutes
Science Citation rates and the journal impact factor for health related publications at selected research institutes
Number of international accreditations received

Improved quality and effectiveness of government and private health systems.

Indicators:
# of hospitals accredited
% hospitals compliant with minimum standards of care
% laboratories doing cross-check for QA

District capacity, leadership and health governance improved in a decentralized, district-led system.

Indicators:
# of districts budgeting at least X% for health programs
districts engaging civil society in health system oversight

Effective programs leveraged for impact at scale.

Indicators:
# of PMDT sites operating at scale
# of women receiving AMTSL

Critical Assumptions

- No catastrophic natural disasters that will require a significant resource shift away from GHI implementation
- Indonesia will continue to experience economic growth and a positive shift towards a full democracy
- Indonesia and the US will continue moving forward in good faith on the Comprehensive Partnership

Annex Three: Indonesia GHI Country Strategy Matrix

Relevant National Priorities/ Initiatives: All GHI activities support the Indonesia 2010-2014 National Medium-Term Development Plan and/or the Millennium Development Goals (MDG)

Overall GHI Principles: All activities implemented through GHI support the following GHI Principles

- Encourage Country Ownership and Invest in Country Led Plans and
- Increase Impact through Strategic Coordination and Integration

Priority Actions with Largest Impact	Key Partners
Focus Area 1: Catalyze action to accelerate Indonesia's progress toward achievement of MDGs 4, 5 & 6	
Additional Key GHI Principles: • Focus on Women, Girls and Gender Equality • Build Sustainability through Health Systems Strengthening • Strengthen and Leverage Other Efforts • Accelerate Results through Research and Innovation	
MDG 4&5 – Child and Maternal health	
Improved management of complications and quality of clinical care in facilities and referrals Integrated Maternal/child health, malaria in pregnancy and immunizations in Eastern Indonesia Zinc scale up for treatment of childhood diarrhea and improved management of acute respiratory infections	MOH, UNICEF, Jhpiego, pharmaceutical industry, WHO, PDUI, IBI
Partnership on hospital accreditation	MOH, WHO, JCI
Technical assistance to immunization program, measles elimination, Support for polio elimination/eradication, expand RED approach, introduce new vaccines	MOH, WHO, UNICEF
Technical assistance for 2012 Demographic and Health Survey	Macro, BKKBN, BPS, UNFPA
MDG 6 – HIV/AIDS	
HIV/AIDS prevention among high risk groups Capacity building of local organizations and NGOs to reach high risk groups	MOH, National AIDS Commission, FHI, TRG/RTI, GFATM, CSOs, Indonesia Planned Parenthood Association, Nahdatul Ulama, TNI PUSKES
Grant to Indonesia Partnership Fund – for HIV/AIDS	National AIDS Commission, CSOs, GFATM
MDG 6 – Tuberculosis	
With National TB program: support scale up of DOTS, linkages with private sector and hospitals including use of international standards of care, scale up of MDR-TB diagnosis and treatment, TB/HIV and Laboratory strengthening for TB, MDR-TB and AI	MOH, KNCV, WHO, FHI, MSH, ATS, IUATLD, Global Fund
Technical assistance to Indonesian drug manufacturers to obtain WHO prequalification status	MOH, USP and Indonesian pharmaceutical companies
Support to communities for TB	MOH; local NGOs

MDG 6 – Other Major Infectious Diseases	
Technical assistance to MOH to conduct mass drug administration for lymphatic filariasis and soil transmitted helminthes and Support to districts for operational costs for MDAs	MOH,WHO, University of Indonesia, RTI, TBD
Support to National Influenza Center for lab based surveillance, Syndromic surveillance for patients, and Support for Early Warning system for respiratory outbreaks; Enhanced surveillance in East Jakarta	National Institute of Health Research and Development, MOH, MOA, WHO, FAO
Animal surveillance and response Improving cleaning and disinfection throughout poultry supply chain Improved biosecurity and good farming practices at commercial poultry farms	FAO, Ministry of Agriculture, AUSAID, ACAIR, Indonesian Dutch partnership (IDP), JICA.
Behavior change communication to improve community awareness and response	Kemenkokesra, MOA, MOH, FAO, John Snow International, US-CDC, USDA
Commodities and supply for API: PPE, decontamination kits, disinfectants, sample collection kits) and Support for lab logistics for AI	John Snow International, MOH, MenkoKesra, Ministry of Agriculture, law enforcement, TNI.
Field epidemiology training	WHO, FAO, MOH, US-CDC, , Indonesian Universities, MOA, DAI, US Universities, TRG, Ecology and Environment, Inc,

Focus Area 2: Enhancing the Use of Quality Research and Evidence in Policy and Programming

Additional Key GHI Principles:
- Build Sustainability through Health Systems Strengthening
- Strengthen and Leverage Other Efforts
- Accelerate Results through Research and Innovation
- Promote Learning and Accountability through Monitoring and Evaluation

IR 2.1 Improved availability of good quality data for programming and policies to improve public health.	
Disease surveillance & Prevalence Surveys 　Detect ILI, SARI, Febrile Illness cases 　Diagnosis and treat TB and MDR TB 　TB Prevalence Survey 　NTD mapping and prevalence data 　Indonesia Demographic Health Survey 　AI prevalence survey and risk assessments 　Building capacity in applied epidemiology through Field Epidemiology Training 　Disease Burden Study for Pneumococcal prevalence	MOH; local NGOs, National Institute of Health Research and Development, MOA, WHO, FAO, AUSAID, ACAIR, IDP, JICA.
Operational Research, Public Health surveys and studies 　Integrated Biological Behavior Surveillance (IBSS) (Papua) 　Operational Research to understand barriers for condom use 　Health Seeking Behavior Surveys for Avian influenza 　TB Operational Research and support the National TB OR Working Group 　Investigation of AI vaccine efficacy in poultry 　Oxytocin Potency Assessment 　Magnesium Sulfate survey- Management of Pre-	MOH, CSOs, Indonesia Planned Parenthood Assoc., Nahdatul Ulama, Kemenkokesra, MOA, FAO, ACIAR, AusAID, IDP, EU, Indonesian Science academy and US National Academy of Sciences, JHPIEGO, Save the Children, JSI, USP

eclampsia and Eclampsia • Partnership between Indonesian Science academy and US National Academy of Sciences	
Develop data collection and tracking systems • E-TB manager system to track MDR treatment and drug supplies • Supply chain assessments (AI, TB, and HIV) • Novel tools for data collection/management • Establish an integrated health data repository • Strengthening Health Information Systems • Local area monitoring and tracking support routine MCH data • Support for Dashboard implementation for Global Fund CCM and principle recipients	MOH, UNICEF, Coordinating Ministry for People Welfare, CSOs, GFATM CCM and PRs, WHO, IDI, IDAI, AUSAID and EU
Enhancing Laboratory Capacity • Risk assessments for laboratory biosafety and biosecurity • Laboratory renovations • Extensive training for laboratory personnel • Laboratory management training • Introducing new methodologies and technologies	MOA, Min of Research & Development, Eijkman Institute, MOH; KNCV, WHO, FHI, MSH, ATS, IUATLD, JSI, MenkoKesra, law enforcement, TNI, University of Gadjah Mada; U.S. Universities
IR 2.2 New technologies and innovations introduced to impact public health outcomes.	
Improving accuracy and efficiency of disease diagnosis • Xpert for more accurate and rapid MDR TB testing • New methodologies and tools to detect emerging diseases • Rapid diagnostics for malaria testing at the village level • Gold standard testing for Neglected Tropical Diseases • HAIN Test study for MDR TB testing • International techniques to rapidly diagnosis and sequence influenza viruses	NIHRD, MOH, KNCV, WHO, FHI, MSH, ATS, IUATLD, University of Indonesia, RTI, FAO, OIE, EU, AUSAID.
Enhancing communication to demand public health services and to save lives • new technologies to improve communication at the community level to increase demand for quality services • computer based Resource Estimate Tools for Advocacy (HIV)	National AIDS Commission, MOH, Jhpiego, CSOs, GFATM
Improving treatment and care to increase patient survival • Oxygen therapies to treat ARIs • Active Management of Third Stage Labor • Support roll out of AMTSL and MgSO4 for PPH and Eclampsia management • Kangaroo mother care	Mercy Corps, MOH, UNICEF, Jhpiego
Build capacity to roll out new technologies and innovations (e.g. Early Warning Alert and Response system- provided training, technical assistance, and web-based database)	WHO, MOH, Jhpiego, Professional organizations, AUSAID and EU
IR 2.3 Expanded and improved quality health research.	
Increase basic and applied research in public health fields and Create local capacity to develop new and test medical products • Track influenza antigen shift and use data to develop new vaccines and promote rational use of	WHO, UNICEF, FAO, OIE, MOH, EU, AUSAID.

vaccines • Detecting newly emerging diseases • In-depth review of measles vaccine program	
Support international partnerships and improve standards/quality • Partnerships for Enhanced Engagement in Research (NAS and NSF) • NIAID partnership with NIHRD • Joint National Academies report Reduction MMR and NMR in Indonesia • Clinical Research Network • Support public-private partnerships to increase innovation and Research & Development	WHO, FAO, OIE, MOH, EU, AUSAID, Indonesian Universities, MOA, DAI, US Universities, TRG, Ecology and Environment, Inc., HKI, Indonesian Academy of Science, U.S. Nat'l Academy of Science

Focus Area 3: Partnering to Address Regional and Global Infectious Disease Threats

Additional Key GHI Principles:
- Build Sustainability through Health Systems Strengthening
- Strengthen and Leverage Other Efforts
- Accelerate Results through Research and Innovation
- Promote Learning and Accountability through Monitoring and Evaluation

R 3.1 Improved preparedness and ability to respond to global and regional infectious disease threats.	
Improved implementation of infectious disease programs of global regional significance in accordance with international standards (TB, API, HIV, EPT, EPI, malaria, polio and measles) Develop and test model regional approaches and technologies for rapid impact on global/regional ID threats (PMDT, GenXpert , RDMA lab network, local manufacturers pre-qualified for 2nd line drug manufacturing)	MOH, USP, Coordinating Ministry for People Welfare, CSOs, Indonesia Planned Parenthood Association, Nahdatul Ulama, FAO, MOA, USDA, AUSAID, ACAIR, IDP, JICA; KNCV, WHO, FHI, MSH, ATS, IUATLD,
Improved diagnostic capacity for targeting and monitoring program implementation (lab strengthening for AI, TB, NTD)	MOH; local NGOs, WHO, University of Indonesia, RTI, National Institute of Health Research and Development, FAO, OIE, NIHRD, US-CDC, EU, AUSAID.
R 3.2 Increased commitment to and leadership in global health priorities.	
Engagement of health leaders in global strategic initiatives and dialogue (GAELF board membership, RDMA lab network, GenXpert roll-out) Improved compliance with global standards for disease control, surveillance	MOH, USP, NIHRD, NIADI, WHO, University of Indonesia, RTI, FAO, Ministry of Agriculture, IDP, AUSAID, ACAIR, JICA, OIE, , and EU.
Improved surveillance capacity (TA for bio-risk; support for clinical trials; EPT, SMS gateway)	MOH, MOA, Ristek, Indonesian Academy of Sciences, Min of Research & Development, Eijkman Institute, WHO, FAO, OIE, EU AUSAID.